by the same author

A Body Of Water

BODY IN SOUL

Wadiz

First published in 2021
by A. Moon & Son Publishing
3 Hood, Dartington, Devon TQ9 6AB

Technical support from francisporterdesign.com

*The Key:
for complete song-sheets, with notated melodies and chords,
go to soundsofwings.com.*

ISBN   978-1-5262-0900-9

INDEX

Part 1

CHILD
Whose Questions Are Those?   4
Venice   10
Donkeys Do Not Seek Solitude   12
Take Your Time   16
Has The Attention Span Of A Gnat   17
Humanity Needs Your Presence Now   18
Hare, Rama and Bodhisattva   21

BREAD
The Giant Red Button   26
The Surface Of The Blue Planet   28
We Who Remain   29
Not Reading   30
Your Functions Are Unkempt   32
Your Love Is For Them   34
Pondering   36
I Bow To Change   38
Of Course We Know   40
Until We Die Of It   42

HOME
Gull   46
Who Do You Think?   48
Just After Two   50
The Three Gurus   50
Basset Hounds Run Past   51
Poetic Quartet #1   52
We Try Not To Think About It   53
What I'd Like To Do On A Sunday   54
I Tell Myself   55
?AIC   55
The New Game   56

Part 2

UNKNOWN
Prologue   60
Zero   61
The Point Being?   61
Biology Test #1   62
After Me   62
Who Took?   63
What????   63
Taste The Freedom   64
Different Angles   66
And I dreamed That I Would Wake Up   68

FLOWING
This River Is Not A River   72
El Loco Colón   74
Ripples On The Water   77
She Is Love   78
What The Crocus Told Me   80
Special Celebration   82
God And Me   84

PEACEFUL MIND
A Prayer Of Welcoming   88
A Prayer Of Thanks For
   The Ability To Make Choices   89
A Prayer Of Relaxation   90
Prayer Of Living Faith   93
In Praise Of The Silent Sound:
   Prayer Of The Holy Wow   94
This Is Enough   96
I Feel This And I Know It   98
(To exist is to be now)   99
The Practice Of Love   100
Interbeing Invocation   101
Everything I Know   104

THE KEY
Look Again And See 108
All We Can Say 109
The Garden Of The Heart 110
You Make Your Life 112
Weary Traveler 114
Of Woman 116
Beauty 118
Surrender My Heart 119
Yes There Is No Path 120
The Flower Of Love 122
Attune Your Receptivity 124
Unmoor Your Boat 126
Keep It Simple 128
This Is It 130
Love Is The Answer 132
In Love With Life 133
With This Sacred Breath 134
Here Are The Stars 135

Photo Credits 139

Epilogue 141

This Is Her World

Do you want to improve your life
And other people's lives,
Make the world a better place?
If yes, then
You would be stopping the desecration of nature
And of nature's ways.
You would be moving towards your way of life
Being harmonious with nature's ways.
Because you are not separate from nature.
This planet, this universe, is one system.
If you think it can be improved, you are mistaken.
Look again.
If you think technology can improve it, look again.
Sunshine, air, water, earth, plants, life,
These are the sacred things ~
No machines, no robots or computers could ever
Replace them.
The sacred we need, the sacred we are.
Anything contrary is suicidal.

When you need any help,
Go to nature, be with nature,
Observe closely and commune deeply,
She provides everything,
She made you,
This is Her world that we are living in.

Wai Ting Li
(b.1923)

CHILD

Whose Questions Are Those?

~

Ever since I was a child, I have had unbidden memories of some previous incarnation or other. One came to me this morning as I was stepping out of my front door. I will tell you about it. The time is probably five or six hundred years before now, early spring, the snows have gone and the farmers are in the fields all day. My name is Li Bo Xi, I am a local government official, in a small town in southern China. I have two daughters and my wife is expecting again. I am praying for a son. I am walking the track that follows our river, going upstream to call on the retired General Wang. He has recently moved into a fine old house and my duty is to finalise arrangements for his welcoming dinner with Town Councillor Fu Chen. The nearest city is a journey of three days, there is a mayor there and I know of no-one of a higher rank outside the capital. I am studying every night for my next exams. If I am to provide adequately for my family I must advance.

Unfortunately there are no suitable positions here unless Fu Cheng were to die, which I do not wish for. The priest has been teaching me about karma so I understand it is only such merit as is worthy in the eyes of God that determines one's destiny in the next life. These burdens lie heavily on my spirit, and I wonder what does God make of that? To attain the rank I want, moving to the city is a necessary evil, and I know nothing of their ways. I hear the officials there are like a pack of wolves and I cannot see but that they would make short work of me.

So preoccupied am I with these thoughts that when I look

up and see a man on the riverbank I am so startled, I stumble. He is sitting with his head in his hands and a heavy bag on the ground beside him. As I tighten my grip on my bamboo cane I notice next to him a wooden staff leaning against a tree. I have a wild idea that he is the General, whom I have not yet seen, although I have heard he is unusually tall. I have to pass close to this fellow. Getting nearer, I see he is small and gaunt. I have also heard that the General has brought with him a small retinue of old soldiers who now constitute his household, taking the places of gardeners, cooks, guards and servants. Somehow I am sure this man is not one of them. I remember too that the other member of the General's party is a widowed niece, and that I have heard whispers about this woman. And as for the general himself, he might be considered somewhat arrogant in his eccentricities were it not for his distinguished military record. I am now about to address the stranger and I realise with an uneasy jolt that my official responsibilities may require me to question him. He could be a criminal on the run. If, later on, he proves to be a danger to the community I would be answerable. I address him thus:

"Excuse me please, good sir, for intruding, but I couldn't help wondering if you were in some distress, and if I might be of service to you?"

I feel very displeased with these words, even as I am speaking them. I feel quite distinctly that I am setting in motion a hitherto dormant wheel of karma, yet also that I am powerless to stop myself. I can only observe in horror as events unfold, as if I am suddenly tumbling down a steep hill, sharply aware of my mortality and insignificance.

The stranger lowers his hands slowly, raises his head, and our eyes meet. There is something about his face. Had we been friends at school? Many years have passed since then.

"You are very kind, but the burden is no-one's but my own."

He is the most extraordinarily pitiful soul. At this moment I could withdraw respectfully and we would go our separate ways, never to meet again. But it seems I am bound, tied hand and foot to the wheel which continues its sickening rotation, as unstoppable as the tides of the seas, or destiny itself. And so I ask him,

"I beg you to forgive my curiosity but I cannot help observing the unusual size and shape of your sack and I confess I am anxious to know, if you'll permit, what it contains."

The stranger regards me with pale, unblinking eyes.

"Questions," he says. "For many years I have been accumulating questions, unanswered questions that is, and they are in this sack and I will carry them all until either they are answered or I take them to my grave."

I could not believe him, I could not understand it, this sack filled with questions, and I could not help a little smile of bemusement, although I regretted it acutely when I saw his own expression harden in response.

"Oh yes, my friend," he said, with great bitterness. "You are not the only one who thinks I am absurd!"

"Forgive me, please, I - "

"Open it, if you want to see with your own eyes!"

"No, no, of course - "

"Open it!"

He pushed the sack towards me and it toppled over at my feet. I reached down, untied the knot in the drawstring and opened the mouth of the sack. Hundreds of strips of cloth were there, and upon each one was a handwritten question.

"Take one, read it!"

I thrust in my hand, pulled one out and read aloud.

" 'When will I die?' "

"Ha!" the stranger made a cheerless laugh. "Perhaps I will know the answer to that one soon enough! Pick another!"

I thrust my hand to the bottom of the sack.

" 'How do thoughts arise?' "

"You see!" he cried. "That is worth asking, is it not? I see clearly in your face that you agree. Another!"

" 'Is it possible for me to control the passage of time?' "

After this I paused, wanting to choose my next words carefully.

"Take another, if you like, read them all!" the stranger said.

"No thank you. I have no doubt they are all excellent questions. But I would like to know if a certain question in my mind is also in your sack."

With a barely perceptible tilt of his head, he indicated that I should continue.

"My question," I said, "is this: why is it necessary to carry this sack with you? Can you not simply accept that these questions are without answers?"

He gave out a kind of grunt which expressed disdain very clearly.

"That is not in the sack because I have the answer to it. But you, my friend, are missing the point! You have your sack of questions too, oh yes, not a visible one, not a physical one, but you carry it all the same, questions that you have asked and that you have not answered. I am glad you do not try to deny it, if you did, our conversation would be at an end. The point is, in my sack it is not only that there are unanswered questions, but every one of them I have personally examined to the limit of my powers. Whereas in your sack there are questions that you have not examined fully, there are questions you don't even know you are carrying, and I can assure you that your collection is a far greater burden than mine."

"And if I were to take your sack and throw it into the river?"

"Ridiculous, stupid fellow! Do you pretend to not hear what I am telling you? Your sack is in your head!"

"You believe you are at liberty to mock me," I replied. "Allow me to inform you that I am an amateur storyteller and you are nothing more than a character in one of my stories. I invented you, I created you!"

The stranger threw his head back and laughed with unrestrained pleasure.

"So, you have made up a story with yourself as a character in it, and you think that gives you control over everything and everybody? Ridiculous! Absurd! You are no different from me, you are not the author, you are a version of him, an imitation. He can never be in this world, just as we can never be in his."

"How can you be so sure?"

The stranger looked troubled at this, and we remained unmoving and in silence for some time. At last he said,

"All right, I accept this as a fair exchange: I have brought your attention to the existence of your own sack of questions, albeit an invisible, mental sack, and you have given me a question to add to mine. I thank you and bid you good day."

I bade him good day likewise and feeling somewhat relieved to quit his company, I walked away. However I could not resist one glance back and saw him writing on a strip of cloth, which he then thrust into the sack. He tightened and knotted the drawstring, lifted the sack onto his back, and set off downstream. I watched him briefly and then returned to my own way, shaking my head with a wry chuckle as I wondered what the wording of the new question he had written might have been.

Venice

~

So many stories made up your life.
How many before you can accept the reality of this life?

The attempts you make to reduce the infinite to a level of comprehension - these are part of the infinite;
even now as you attempt to reconcile, on your mental plane, your notion of the infinite with the true infinite.

Perhaps you find some peace in saying,
    "Well, I accept that these are, by definition, unreconcilable, and I reconcile myself to this acceptance."

And yet wanting is not having: the peace you yearn for is not here, so you suppose you will go mad, even though you don't know what that means, but if you haven't been to Venice, you don't know what going to Venice actually is, although you may imagine it, or read about it, or see pictures or watch films about it.

Or you could write 'Venice' on paper boats and play with them in the bath.

So see if you can go mad without knowing whether you will be able to return to sanity because, well, it's no secret: the hidden agenda of the exercise at this stage is that you will not be able to come back.

And the whole point of the exercise at this point is to realise that you won't want to come back; it will be both a virtual impossibility and something that no sane person would choose anyway.

Your sanity, such as it now is, is your prison, and one of the strongest locks on the door is you saying to yourself,
   "Ho ho ho! I know all about my sanity, such as it now is, being a prison!"

It takes seeing how locked in you are and feeling how much you are longing for freedom, to begin. At the end.

‡

Donkeys Do Not Seek Solitude

~

Donkeys do not seek solitude. This is a widely accepted fact, even among those whose paths have not yet lead them to any personal acquaintance with any donkey. Such people are, of course, in the majority and, until yesterday afternoon, I had been happy to count myself among their number. Thus when, for the first time in my life, whilst taking a constitutional stroll in nearby woodland, into my line of vision befell a living, breathing donkey, my initial association was not, as one might have expected, with the famous Biblical passage, but with the aforementioned general knowledge that donkeys have inclinations to gregariousness. Noting at once that this particular specimen was clearly solitary, I freely admit to straight away feeling slightly alarmed, a feeling which very soon increased as it also broke in upon me that I found myself in close proximity to an actual animal that had, until then, existed only in my idle imaginings.

So suddenly sharpened, in fact, were my senses that it was all in an instant that I beheld in detail the height, the weight, the hooves, the idiot expression, and I immediately began, in spite of myself, speculating upon the possible size of a part of the anatomy not at that moment presented to my view, namely, the teeth. I further attest to a sudden acute dread, and simultaneously an absolute conviction, that some species of foul play had recently occurred, in which the donkey's part was central. A little deeper in the woods a body would be discovered in the bracken, hoof prints in the blood-stained mud. The open sky was a glorious blue!

As I attempted to assess the situation, the beast shambled closer, apparently unconcerned by my presence. This indifference was, to me, a tactical bluff. At this point in time a distance of some ten or twelve metres lay between us; the path was wide enough for only one to pass, thickly leaved trees and thorny brambles loomed impenetrably on all sides. The beast paused to tug with its mouth at some foliage in the verge, all the while keeping its cold eye on me. Something now stirred within my soul. I felt the basic urge to turn and flee but swiftly mastered it. I felt the rising of an ancient nobility of spirit, the pride of a hunter, the most refined form of courage that is called upon perhaps only once or twice in the lives of those whose fate it is to face the ultimate test.

Thus I stood my ground. I lifted my chin to the aggressor, the beast, the demon. I was filled with determination to meet the moment. The rogue donkey finished eating and came on again. I saw its shoulders squaring up, I saw its eyes redden and its teeth snarl. I saw it grow in size and gain in speed. I set myself firm, raised my fists, my own roar ready to rise, and the animal came on, right at me, I heard its blowing breath, its hooves stamping the earth. Then it was all upon me, I reached out, felt the course, greasy hair of its stocky neck rasping between my fingers as it bundled me aside but somehow, as I fell, I was able to summon the necessary strength, agility and co-ordination to strike a resounding blow on the passing rump with the flat of my hand.

I crashed to the ground amidst a tangle of twigs and thorns, my view of the retreating challenger obscured by the undergrowth in which I now found myself restrained. Lying still for a deliberate few seconds, I was aware of a sudden quiet, and the fading sound of distant pounding hooves.

I picked myself up, brushed myself down and peered along the track. No sign of another living creature, although crows now cawed raucously overhead. I shook off the tilth from my trousers and set off once more, with a spring in my stride, along the familiar path through the woodland I loved so well!

‡

Take Your Time

~

People are always telling me to take my time, but they never say where from. They mean well though, so I don't ask. It's just a (so-called) figure of speech. Taking such things too literally can be, well, a waste of time. So, I will take my time. After all, I keep getting offered new bits of it.

‡

Has The Attention Span Of A Gnat

~

This phrase is used to express a feeling about someone, a feeling that is more or less dismissive, derogatory and snide. It has been made to work as a comedy line too sometimes, but this only adds force to the point I want to make. Behind the words is an attitude towards gnats that is thoughtless, careless, yet widely accepted. Embrace the pedantic here briefly, if you will, and consider:

What do you actually know about the attention span of a gnat? *[Practically nothing.]*

When did you last even see one?
[I don't remember. Remind me what they look like?]

The power of the collective unconscious is increasing. Are you willing to look at the nature of your unique contribution to that power? And to be fully responsible for it? Answering these questions is an eminently suitable use of the attention span of a human being.

It could well be also a requirement, for survival and liberation, yours individually and all life globally.

‡

Humanity Needs
Your Presence Now

~

I Feel It

There is a stage in the natural course of its development when your mind, without you knowing it, is constantly devising and refining strategies for its own survival. These include: demanding energy and attention; hiding its own limitations; believing that it can, in time, understand and explain everything. Yet the nature of my consciousness, of my existence, is more than I can ever grasp with my mind alone. *The Tao that can be named is not the Tao*. Perhaps the best anyone can say about consciousness is 'I feel it', in the sense of feeling being greater than understanding.

You And Me

The individuality of you and me is generally taken for granted. From the point of view of consciousness things look different, although these words are inadequate and misleading because to have a point of view implies subject and object, and such divisions don't apply in the realm of consciousness, where there is no doing, only being; no time or space, only is-ness. This is where the miraculous, wondrous and unique nature of human being opens up: to be able to know and experience both the Two-ness of individuality and the Oneness of All.

Experience The University

In normal life, a typical mind is working hard on a hidden agenda to resist any moves towards realisation of full consciousness, of feeling presence. And there are good reasons for this. Given that everything is connected, any (and every) experience you have is as complex as the entire universe; no experience can be repeated, recreated or translated. From there it follows that A) all your memories are not simply inaccurate, they are malleable versions of the reality; and B) the notion of 'the reality' is itself no more than an idea. The mind is very reluctant to admit that being conscious is much more than having a mind.

From the ego's devotion to its self-constructed identity (which in reality is a delusion) arise not just opinions and preferences, but all the heartless, greedy and cruel actions that have ever been, from making a tactless comment to the ignorant destruction of the ecological systems upon which all life depends. An unrestrained ego is separation personified; anti-connection, anti-interdependence personified.

Humanity Needs Your Presence Now – Note To Self

Living from presence is being truly human; living from and making decisions from mind/ego without presence is anti-human, it is actively against life itself.

A willingness to learn and practice quieting the mind, to end the mind's separation agenda as the dominant force in your life – thus making space for presence – this is fundamental and essential to being genuinely in service to both your own humanity, to humanity at large, and to all life.

Hare, Rama and Bodhisattva

~

I asked my friend Raima, because I reckoned she knew something, about the meaning of the words Hare, Rama and Bodhisattva. This is what she told me.

"They are words from the version of Buddhism in India. Now as you know I'm not a Buddhist scholar, I'm not any kind of scholar, and not much of a Buddhist either in fact, so this is my interpretation not a translation.

So Hare, this is a kind of greeting. Looking at the whole spectrum of greetings, near one end we have, "Hi there, how you doin'?" the Joey from Friends one, and a bit further along there's the Kim Jong Il from Team America World Police one, "Harrow, I'm so Ronry." Then several million places further along at the other end, we have Hare, which can be thought of as the verbal equivalent of bowing. Not just a nod of the head though, because you're acknowledging the Supreme Being and that often means this tsunami sized wave of love and light that is too bright to look into with your eyes open, so if you just nod your head, it comes off in the blast of light, yes, your head comes off thanks to the Supreme Being. So this is when you opt instead, probably, for full prostration so that the light-wave can wash over you and through you. That's Hare.

Rama is just one of many names for the Supreme Being (Ram is another) who is in fact unnameable. There are gods everywhere in India. The Supreme Being is sometimes also called the God of the gods. The thing about that is, not the king of the gods, not the chief god, but the God of the gods, you see, a complete shift of dimension. To give you another example of the kind of shift of dimension I'm talking about, imagine a friend has been pondering the problem of chicken and egg, which came first and all that, she's been trying to work it out all night, and you've just been sleeping through, maybe drooling on the pillow a bit, and by the morning she's been thinking so much her brains have turned into scrambled egg and she's sitting at the kitchen table with a sign round her neck which says, Eat Me. Well, Freud would probably be very excited by that story but he's not here tonight. And so we come to bodhisattva.

Now the standard answer to what is a bodhisattva is not really very good, because it will tell you that a bodhisattva is a kind of saint, someone who was able to attain nirvana but, out of a deep compassion for all humanity, turns back to the world with a mission to ease suffering wherever they go. The deep compassion bit I think is accurate because one person cannot attain nirvana if other people are suffering and anyway the Rig Veda, a very old mystical text, puts it like this: all beings are, by their very existence, enlightened. Enlightenment isn't an idea, it's a real happening thing. In the Eternal Now there is no future, and if there's no future you're not going to get enlightened next week, or next year or even in your next moment, because if you're going to be enlightened it can only be now, it's just that your idea of what enlightenment is is unlikely to match what it really is. So in a nutshell a bodhisattva is someone who loves life and lives for love."

‡

BREAD

The Giant Red Button

~

So this is how that stodgy white plastic-wrapped bread is made. I'm given a white coat, a white hat, a hairnet and ear-plugs, I've become one of the bread ants. As the noise in here is too much for talking, the supervisor shouts instructions into my ear, just like he has to an unmemorable number of other new recruits before me, like a human machine would do it, and I don't blame him, this is a factory, it could be an aircraft hangar but it's filled with machines that run twenty-four hours a day, I glimpse a couple of guys with tools in the metal guts of one, I get the impression if anything breaks it's immediately fixed and set going again. Relentlessness is thick in here. I check the recipe chart again and start my job: heave a sack of the right type of flour off the pallet, pull it to the mixer-bowl, just like a kitchen mixer but a giant version, an extraordinary sight, pull the string to open the sack, lift it over the brim, tip it in, bin the empty sack, measure the water, keep track of what's gone in, some sacks are not to be emptied fully but measured, I must check the weight and finally push the giant green button and the machine starts mixing, and it's powerful, if I fell in there it would do me in for sure in no time, so this is working in a factory, only eleven hours and twenty-five minutes before I can go home, and then back tomorrow, I really don't know if I can do this, the constant noise is intense, but all these others are doing it, one of them saw 'first shift' all over me and said 'good money' with a passing grin, I'm one of the few white guys here, the supervisor appears, he beckons me away, I follow, threading a way through the throng of throbbing metal things all much higher and bigger and more important than me, heat, flour-dust and sweat in the air, was I no good at the mixing? he stations me at a slicing machine, part of a conveyor track made of grey metal slats that channels the loaves in, the slicer shudders through then the sliced loaf is shunted into the bagging machine that another white-coated and hatted and netted person is watching, we just watch our machines until there's a blockage, hypnotised in no time, repetition of mechanics, the bread looks so ugly, not like food, more like the waste products of the robot we're within, the garish plastic packaging is telling a lie, of course it would be like this but now I've seen it for myself, I'm here for the money, is it worth it? and I wish I was somewhere else for something else, but there's eleven hours and ten minutes before I can go home, I could walk out but that would be wrong, but no-one here would care, would they? if I was more of a man I wouldn't have ended up here, Jesus, Marxism is a lot more meaningful, I feel my spirit shrinking, eleven hours and five minutes to go and then back again tomorrow, how can I do this, I need the money to buy food and run the car so that I can get here, it is a level of hell, I'm in it and I'm staying, I want to weep but there's a blockage, it's my turn to move, it's a relief to have something to do, I push the giant red button.

‡

The Surface of the Blue Planet

~

From the polystyrene-tiled ceiling
fluorescent tubes stab down numbing pain.
A cathode-ray TV, in a blister of shadow, is buzzing
so loud it's almost spitting, as if with barely suppressed rage.
Transistorised sound pollution
seeping pop through the wall, insane, frivolous,
as happy as a robot clown.
On the screen old images of war,
condensed noises of gunfire and explosions,
pictures and sound in black and white,
as shiny and cold as a knife in the gutter.
Colour pictures appear, lifeless, lurid,
the thickly painted face of a corpse.
A black electric flex crosses the floor,
an umbilical cord joining the TV to its feed socket in the wall.
Within the wall more wires hiss in straight lines
back to their rigid lung the fuse box,
through the fuses into the main cable,
thick under the asphalt, under oblivious street traffic,
to the sub-station, through transformers heavier than trucks,
and up into the grey steel grip of the pylon line,
and away across fields,
away to the power station itself
where the turning of turbines makes the very ground vibrate,
where billions of electrons jostle and mass
and leap across vast divides,
ordered by immortal forces,
marshalled by the will of some of those that dwell
on the surface of the blue planet.

We Who Remain

~

Some are gone,
The rest stay on:
We, who may speak of The Departed
In words great, or small,
Or not speak, or even think, of Them at all.

Speaking 'of' and 'to' are worlds apart;
Our words are [as much] amongst Us
As They are not.

How much more than the thoughts of others
Are we now, though we remain?
Are we much less fleeting?

For with the end of Our time and space,
Then what will Their words and thoughts
Of Us be to Us!

The only matter: to love
This time, this space, this life,
As [if there were] no present, no gift, like it.

‡

Not Reading

I am not reading the words in the following line
in reverse order.
No, I am definitely not going to do that.

But having said that
(I'm really not so sure whether I said it or read it,
or if someone else did)
I'm really not so sure if it's true.

Wonder I this to point a is there if.

‡

Your Functions Are Unkempt

Your placebo effect is red,
your placenta is a belief system,
your maternal instincts are tractable,
your pencil is a prayer,
your ineffability is flipping marvellous,
your instructors are impoverished.

Your tractor is warm,
your teapot is noisy,
your table is timed,
your time is planed,
your air is unknown,
your whereabouts are invisible.

Your vision is reciprocal,
your telepathy is unclouded,
your question is whether,
your systems are informed,
your functions are unkempt,
your winnings are repeated.

Your positions are in metals,
your string is a bamboo pole,
your promises are structural,
your exits are trophies,
your drivers are meddling,
your destinations are indiscreet.

Your pleasures are refracted,
your creations are rebellious,
your curtains are falling,
your fingers are flashing like diamonds,
your eyelashes are dripping,
your table is a river of leaves.

Your bath is an elephant,
your best friend is a wet-suit,
your fasting is a fiefdom.

‡

Your Love Is For Them

Stop wasting your time
A bad habit does you no good
The Creator gave you a miracle
This one of being alive

A bad habit is like a vampire
You let it live on your heart
Have more respect for yourself
For your power and for your life

Any power you have
Comes direct from God
Is that a useless thing
To carelessly ignore?

Stop flogging that dead horse
And instead admit
You need a new horse
So get a better one

Take good care of it
With love and respect
Call it 'My Inspiration'
Enjoy riding every day

Please bury your dead
Before they start to stink
Some habits are so old
The bad smell reaches heaven

Don't be offensive
You share this place
You have neighbours
Your love is for them.

‡

Pondering

~

I am pondering

Not wondering
I am pondering what to do with my life
That's what I'm doing

I'm doing it
Pondering pondering
Pondering pondering

That's what I'm doing with my life
I am pondering

Pondering what to do
With my life.

‡

I Bow To Change

~

The ground is dark
The air is frozen
The sky is hard

I do all I know
To stay alive

Is there any change,
Is there any light?
The Earth is turning
The light is returning

There are no pauses
There is this changing
Of everything flowing in its own time
From darkness to all colours
From all colours to darkness

Here a planet rotating
And on its surface
Embodiments of consciousness
(I am of them)
And a sun being orbited
And a moon orbiting
And stars reaching out
To the insides of infinity

The sky is changing
lightening
The air is changing
warming
The ground is changing
softening

Existing is changing
What I am becoming is unknown
I know what I am
I am bound to change

I bow to change.

‡

Of Course We Know

~

Of course we know
Everyone gets back
Whatever they give out
That is simple resonance

Therefore with love, I give myself
Wholeheartedly
To the truth of being alive
Just as I am now

It's how life is
How do you love?
Show me how
Let me see now

Anyway, you cannot hide
Even your most shameful secret
Why pretend I don't know
Even your darkest desire?

As for your most pathetic weakness
It's nothing special, let me tell you!
And what about your oldest, deepest wound
The one you guard like a dragon with its hoard!

How long are you going to keep
Insisting that it can't be healed?

Bring it all into the light
Nothing is hidden from God

Do you still cling to that old belief
That no-one else can feel as you do?

Being together is growing together
Being together is loving each other

Making the houses of ourselves
Into good homes
For Love and Truth
To live and grow.

‡

Until We Die Of It

~

If your life is like mine,
You don't really know
Your home land,
You don't really know
Your grandparents,

You don't really know
How to live well
Or die well,
You don't really know
Your own heart
Or your soul.

If your life is like mine,
You'll see me weeping
And you won't need to ask why.

If your life is like mine,
I ask you now,
Why are you not weeping?

My dear friend, let us weep together,
Wail and writhe and cry out together,
Until we die of it,

Or learn something new
About love.

HOME

Gull

~

I catch the bus home. It's a single-decker, only one other passenger, sitting in the front section, so I go to the back and take an aisle seat. I'm facing forward, my whole body suddenly goes rigid as I realise there's a large white bird next to me. I don't turn in case it takes flight. I think it's a seagull, in fact I think it's a herring gull by the yellow beak which is clear even in my peripheral vision. No, of course it doesn't have a ticket! If an old person needs the seat I will shoo it away but I sense it is fearful, perhaps injured, perhaps even dying. It has that quality that a dying animal can have, a certain glowing stillness, a sort of dry radiance, like the body straining to stay still to balance a restless fever in the spirit; the preparations for the momentous separation of body and spirit. The person up front hasn't noticed the gull, no-one has noticed it apart from me.

The bus comes to a stop, there's no-one to get on but the other person leaves the bus and without thinking, by habit or reflex, I turn to watch them walking away. I realise I have moved but it's too late. The herring gull, I was right about that, just twitches its neck and stares unblinking, nothing more. Now I can see it. It looks ok, I can't see any injuries. But it's a seagull sitting on a bus! I'm not dreaming! And now I can't turn back but I think that just by me looking at it, it'll get that sense of being prey, so, very slowly, very carefully, I turn to face forward again, but as I do, out of the corner of my eye, I think I see a piece of paper on the gull's seat, under its foot, it can't be a ticket, it can't be! And now it's my stop and, gull or no gull, I have to get home. As I stand up, it's just as if I'm saying 'see you later' to a friend, I glance at the gull, but really just to get another look at the ticket. I couldn't be sure, but it looks like one to me. A gull on the bus now seems pretty normal compared to a gull with a ticket. I get off, the bus pulls away. The window ledge is too high, I can't see if the gull is really sitting there. But it was!

‡

Who Do You Think?

~

Five days ago I was in this very café and I was sitting in this very chair, and who do you think walked in and sat at that table over there, a famous person, somebody everyone would know?

Not everyone would know!

All right, it wasn't the Pope, it wasn't the Second Coming, it wasn't a Scotsman, it wasn't a musician, it wasn't a film star, it wasn't royalty, in fact it wasn't a person at all.

How could it be 'not a person' and everyone knows them?

I didn't mean everyone everyone, I meant everyone who's seen The Life Of Pi.

The Life Of Pi?

The film, not the book.

Look, you said it wasn't a film star!

Well yes, I suppose that was a bit misleading.

You mean to tell me that you were sitting here last week -

Five days ago –

Five days ago, and someone came in who isn't Scottish, or a musician, etc etc and they sat over there and it wasn't a person?

Yes.

You mean to tell me, you expect me to believe, that you saw the tiger from Life Of Pi come in here and sit down? Don't you know it's a CGI tiger? It's not even a real tiger!

Well, it might not have been the same one, but it looked a lot like it.

Was it by itself?

No, there was girl with it.

A girl?

Yes.

A girl and a tiger?

Yes!

A full-grown real tiger.

Yes!

What kind of tea did it have?

Lapsang Souchong.

And what did the girl have?

Milk, just a glass of milk.

Any cake?

Yes, a slice of coffee and walnut, which they shared.

Coffee and walnut cake with Lapsang?

Actually it was obvious they did it for joke, to amuse themselves, they laughed together the whole time.

Tigers don't laugh.

Are you sure? This one did.

Why didn't it eat you?

Don't be daft, it only came in for tea and cake, not a full English.

Do you think they'll ever come back here?

It's funny you should say that - don't look round!

‡

Just After Two

~

I went into town
Just after two,
Had to chase my hat,
Off in the wind it blew.

And a tree came down
In *La Place Des Fous,*
You can guess why that
Made me think of you.

‡

The Three Gurus

~

Spoonerism Guru,
"Which fattles to bite?"

Pirate Guru,
"Oo argh! Oo argh you?"

Sir Real Guru,
"Will milky kebabs?"

‡

Basset Hounds Run Past

~

You might find yourself standing out of doors observing a cloud formation. Your face is upturned for the best view.

You hear a shout, and a strange fast approaching noise,
    "Look out!"
which makes you jump round, and then your airborne feet are hit by a running Basset Hound.

A jump of this nature is a reflex action, an action which occurs prior to an assessment of one's options. As the person jumping, you now have to deal with:

> a) being off-balance at an uncertain height above the ground;
> b) an offended dog that might bite you;
> c) at least one dismayed stranger, possibly of the opposite sex, and
> d) imminent pain from falling to the ground.

You have no time to determine the best thing to do from here, so what you do do is a reflex action, which may or may not be the best thing.

But what happens happens, you just have to deal with it as best you can, Basset Hounds or no Basset Hounds.

‡

Poetic Quartet #1

~

Words

There are no words to express how I feel right now.

Periods

Just as Picasso had his Blue Period, allegedly due to lack of funds he couldn't buy other colours, so I had my Pretentious Period, due to lack of self-awareness and life experience, I imagined I would become a famous poet.

My First Poem

My first poem doesn't properly rhyme,
It's really just one long line,
No, 'rhyme' and 'line' don't really rhyme,
This probably isn't a proper poem
But I wrote it all down
And called it My First Poem
And it takes one big breath to read it all out loud.

My Second Poem

My second poem has three distinguishing features
One of its distinguishing features is
That it over-uses the phrase distinguishing features.
Another of its distinguishing features is
It's non-scanning: a sort of pre-apocalyptic un-poem;
And the third distinguishing feature is it's short
But maybe not really short enough.

We Try Not To Think About It

~

There once was a table and chairs,
They went with the carpet downstairs
While the windows all chanted,
"This roof is so slanted
We no longer think about bears –

Well, we try not to,
We try not to think about bears breaking in."

‡

What I'd Like To Do On Sunday

~

I'd like to have a robot that did the cleaning, cooked a hearty soup and made the bed.

I'd like to have a castle and three dogs, and to ride through the forest like a bad prince.

I'd like to ring the church bell and have everyone running to the church, which would be lined with red velvet cushions, heated to tropical temperatures and the weekly communal sex ritual would ensue.

I'd like to go in drag to the meeting with a tin full of infinite cookies disguised as cupcakes.

I'd like to have more sense than money and then on Monday, vice versa.

‡

I Tell Myself

~

I might tell myself I don't have time for this,
but who would believe me?

‡

?AIC

~

?AIC ecnallievrus ed stob sel sap ehcnelcèd en aç ,siaçnarf ne
eréirra ne sesohc sed erircè'd xueregnad tse'C

‡

The New Game

~

The object of the new game.
Is to improve the satisfaction.
Of all the players.
With their parts in it.

Begin!

‡

UNKNOWN

Prologue

~

There are still in this world some things which are unknown, and others which will forever remain undiscoverable. And although it may initially appear to be irrelevant, here is one of the to-be-discovered things: this same Prologue, which must precede the body of the book, and thus is of course in it's rightful place. However, it must not be denied that the author wrote it after completing the book, not before, for how could a story in all honesty be announced before knowing it oneself? Having laboured at this same Prologue for countless hours, with nineteen out of every twenty draft pages torn out, crumpled and tossed into the fire, like the souls of sinners into damnation, eventually the unfortunate writer came to believe this same Prologue to be among the most lucid, stirring and revolutionary of their entire œuvre, demanding preservation and protection from any insensitive or over-zealous editing, and so it became necessary to perform extensive revisions of the book, in order to bring it into congruence with the glory and magnificence of the Prologue. Similar errors, of style, taste and judgment, are, as you will see, a common theme throughout, but as this is characteristic of most of the actions of humanity, the author begs you to approach with a strong possibility of forgiveness and even of finding merit in the amusement which a cultured and discerning mind (such as, dear reader, your own) can easily derive from examples, of which this book is one, of the heart-rending pathos of entire lives mis-spent in clumsy, ignorant, misguided, yet hard-working, delusion.

Zero

~

one zero
One two one Zero
one two Three two one Zero
one two One zero
one Zero

‡

The Point Being?

~

A paradox reveals the limits
of that particular realm of consciousness.

There are the limits of consciousness,
then what is beyond.

‡

Biology Test #1

~

1. How many years since you first heard about the metamorphosis of the caterpillar?

2. Which one of the following experiences is most different from the others?

    a) You talk with a friend about it.

    c) You read about it in a magazine.

    d) You see a documentary film about it.

    e) You observe the life-cycle of a caterpillar in its natural habitat.

    b) You are a caterpillar.

‡

After Me

~

Unconsciousness, what unconsciousness?
Repeat, what repeat?

‡

Who Took?

~

Who took my time?

‡

What????

~

What is the question, if this is the answer?
If that is the question, then is this the answer?
What if there are no 'what ifs?'
Or was that the answer, because 'what?' was the question?

‡

Taste The Freedom

~

A bit lost? Want a guide, a teacher?

Well, not really, haven't they all been saying the same things
over and over for centuries?
Acknowledge your equality with your neighbour,
recognise it, feel it and live in it.

The roles of teacher and student are interchangeable,
regardless of age or experience.

The path you are on is your path, own it.
You are the guide and the follower,
this moment now is your life and everything you need is here.

(Yeah right, thanks, I've had enough teaching,
I'm off to play!)

Honour the teacher/student,
even when they irritate you greatly,
they want what you want, they're inside you, they are you.

You meet what you meet,
enjoy simply that you are able to meet
the new, the unknown.

A glimpse of the truth that everything is unknown
and a taste of the freedom of this.

You acknowledge your fear, and your courage.

More and more you are moving
with enjoyment and well-being,
in peace of mind and an overflowing heart.

What could be better than respecting reality?
What could be more worthless than denying reality?

What I am feeling now is an integral part of reality.
And every part has its own life, its own way.

And the separation of reality into parts is an illusion!
And all illusions are illusions!

Holy Flip!

Italicised line is from 'Principles of Attitudinal Healing'.

‡

Different Angles

~

Splintered pine-planks fallen cross-angled
off two battered trestles,
the stone floor spread with green paint splashes
in the wood shavings and saw-dust,
the exit sign above the back door lit by an electric bulb
under a trophy stag-head.

Jupiter is singing tunes of foxglove and rye
while Autumn is receiving her dues
from fingers with wedding rings removed,
antlers polished with leather rags,
and black leaves dragged from the bottom of ponds
where no fish live and no people bathe.

The curtains are encrusted with dust webs,
tired old false diamond hoards,
the weight of their own flesh hanging
in imitation of medieval stained-glass windows
depicting scenes of butchery and slaughter,
to instil awe and dread within the flock.

A museum display case of unworn hats,
mirror-tiles arranged at careful random angles behind,
tambura drones faint in the room beyond,
a whiff of dusty perfume,
carpets from the east,
a brass coffee-pot.

The ebony box is tipped on one end,
open lid at right angles,
a mess of pearl necklace, ear-rings and brooches
sprawls across the tabletop
like the ornate drool of a magician's dream.

The clock-tower bell is striking nine in the morning.
As the seventh toll sounds,
a horse rushes into the market square,
no saddle or rider, eyes wide, ears back in frenzy and fear,
hooves scrabbling on the cobbles, scattering boxes,
spilling fruit, flecks of foam fling from its flanks.

A boy grabs an apple and darts out of sight.

‡

And I Dreamed That I Would Wake Up

~

I dreamed I was in a far-off magical land
of colour and aroma, charm and innocence,
all the floors whispered blessings as feet passed over them,
all the walls lived and breathed.

All the pictures were as mirrors, flowers hung from the walls,
all the tables were alive, all the figs were ripe,
all the clocks were panels of moss,
all the cushions fresh as lilies,
all the open windows letting in a balmy air
redolent of tenderness.

I felt refreshed, renewed and re-inspired,
all dutiful tasks were nothing
and I was free to dance through the garden,
fly with the butterflies and drink the best drink ever tasted.

All the waterfalls were just as cooling as should be
on a sunny day,
all the horses wore bells.

All the blades of grass told stories, when asked,
each one a different epic,
and all the clouds played gambling games
with raindrops as chips.

And each and every raindrop was a world in itself
and the ocean was so generous in giving up its mysteries
that nothing could replace it,
and everything was both enough and too much
at one and the same time.

And I dreamed that I would wake up in this world,
and my dream came true!

‡

FLOWING

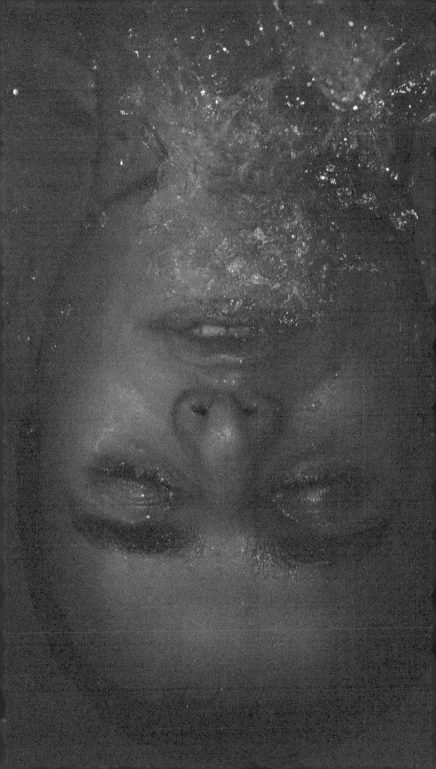

This River Is Not A River

~

Rounded by up-and-over-and-down flowing constant water,
the rocks are a kind of grey that you don't see anywhere else,
so long as you look at it now.

And this river isn't a river really,
it's the pack of fallen leaves in the cleft,
with stories of when the water ran deep
and high and intolerable;
it's the stillness that the quiet trees seem to be guardians of,
and it's the hushed rustling of a bird as it darts away,
sprung from its patch of undergrowth by
rubber boots clomping.

This river is not a river,
it's the wave of grief that washes back
in the wake of the little bird
flying away so fast,
stirring a ripple of childhood,
the agony of a human past.

The air I'm drawing into my chest is cool and damp,
echoes of morning's lifted mist,
I taste the earth as if it were a scented flower.
I feel my own body warm inside my clothes and coat
and woolly hat,
as I stand on the slope and watch
the risen wave that stays as the water goes thrusting through,
moving fast and staying there.

This river is not a river anymore than this walk is a walk
or this breath is a breath.

Everything is an un-nameable THIS
and I thrill in feeling my being here is just like that too.

‡

El Loco Colón

~

Que loco viejo
Y su minúsculo barco
Allí está con él en la arena
El loco Colón, con lo que, aquí

Here was that tiny ship
On this very sand
These same waves, same sea, same sky
That same horizon

Everyone knows his name
First heard it long ago in school
But let's now remember also his crew
Miguel Bautista, Pedro Dasmariñas de María,
Juan de Cuneo, Marco Maduro Lopez, Paulo Sorrente

And all the others
Whose names are lost
Each one taking his own life
In his hands
Over the line

And yet they were not
The first to disappear, nor
The first to show up
One day, out of the blue

Deep transformation
Written all over
Every one of them

With stories that
Had to be told
Had to be heard

I confide in you now
That I, like you, am
One of those nameless

I have returned and
I have stories

The only question
Is shall we
- To share them well -
Give ourselves due time and place
Make ourselves world famous and renowned
Forever
Just for each other?

And going on
More of these fertile forests come into view

How do I value this exchange,
The baring of hearts and souls?

For this, what am I willing to sacrifice?

Together shall we make
This a true act of love
And bear the intimacy,
Eat the fruit of it?

Here, have a taste.

Translation guide
Such a crazy old man
And his tiny boat
There he is with it on the sand
Crazy Columbus, just so

‡

Ripples On The Water

~

Ripples on the water
  Appearing and disappearing
Rain on the river
  Scattering circles on the still surface of the water
Rain coming down on the river making countless ripples
in circles appearing and disappearing on the surface of
the water, now bristling in a breeze.

‡

She Is Love

~

I am never ready
And my beloved is always coming
Always taking me out

My beloved sees the clouds
And knows the sun
She hears my cries of desolation
And my songs of ecstatic praise

She moves now like
Incessant swirling change
And now like
Unceasing certain stillness

Now an eternal living being

My beloved takes me out
Before I put on my best clothes
Takes me dancing before I know the steps
Singing before I know the tune
Before I understand a single word

She loves me before I know what love is
Because
She is love

She is love
And I am like a child
Totally in love
(with playing this game of hide and seek)
with her

Any minute now I'll remember
We are one

And then we'll shake with laughter
In each other's embraces
And tears of joy
Will wet our faces.

‡

What The Crocus Told Me

~

"One of These Petals is wilted,
This Stem has a knot."
Alive Now is the strength and the fragility
perfection is not as real as Reality
no Past or Future but Now
non-judgment, acceptance, Total Acceptance
beyond The Duality
there is no damage or brokenness in the Present
stillness, aliveness, now-ness, new-ness, ness-ness
there is no need for Because, It Is Here,
no need for Trust, no need for Fear
I Am Like This, I am Life like This,
and You Are The Same,
the same sun, the same earth, the same air, the same water
if you're not listening for something, what do you hear,
what is here?
focusing, expanding, contracting, listening, opening,
closing, pulsing, living
extraordinary yes, ordinary yes,
Yes yes no yes, no-ness, now-ness
one, two, many,
one, one, one
always more, always enough, always always,
always beyond always,
beyond beyond
bounding, bouncing, bumping into boundlessness
less-ness, ness-ness
is was shall be

I am one among the many many
I am The One among the many many
You are The One as well, there is only one,
there is no one
it's been said before
it's being now

It's Being Now
How It Is
there aren't really any words for It.

‡

Special Celebration
(or Thanks For My Being)

~

I was in the Deep Dark
Where Time had forgotten how to move
Or perhaps had never known

Nobody knew I was there
No one knew me at all
Not a soul

And then you came
Found me and brought me here

I was wondering how you did it
And when I asked you
You sang me this song

You said, "Words are very narrow
But when you sing them with your heart
Then everything transforms
And everyone is shining with joy

And among other things
This radiance is your guide
In that deep darkness
Where unknown beings dwell

I was once one of them
But now you and I know the truth about each other

Two notes in an endless melody
Two stars twinkling in the boundless heavens
Two raindrops that fell into the ocean

And so simply, gracefully
It comes to us naturally
That we sing and dance together

This is a special celebration
One that goes right through the night."

‡

God And Me

~

Part 1: I Am Not God

I know that God made me
And that I am not God,

But I want so much to know Him.
How could it be otherwise?

So, using what I know,
I imagine what God is like.
How could it be otherwise?

In other words,
I make my God
In my own image.

Yet I know all along
This is not the true God.
How could it be otherwise?

Like the ocean in a raindrop,
I know God is in me,
And I know I am in God,
When I feel my heart,
When my heart is open.

After all, I am talking about
The God of Love.

Part 2: I Am God

I know that I am God
And I know Myself.
How could it be otherwise?

I create imagination
In my own Self,
And then I wonder if
I am not the true Me.
How could it be otherwise?

Like a raindrop in the ocean,
When I feel my heart,
I know love is in me.

When my heart is open,
I know I am in love.
After all,
I am talking about
A human being in Love.

‡

A PEACEFUL MIND

A Prayer Of Welcoming

~

Spirit of peaceful mind
I welcome you
Spirit of trust in love
I welcome you
Spirit of love in action
I welcome you

Please help me make myself a happy home for you all.
So be it.
Thanks be to God.
Amen.

‡

A Prayer Of Thanks For The Ability To Make Choices

~

What a gift it is, the ability to make choices!
I do now make these choices:
I feel total confidence and faith,
I open my whole being to this present reality of aliveness,
I welcome, embrace and rejoice in this new moment of life
I feel loved, blessed and forgiven by
Divine Mother and Father;
I feel protected, guided and arranged for by
My Guardian Angels and spirit guides

I now make the choice to feel as if
all my needs are now met;
all my questions are now answered;
all my problems are now resolved

I now make the choice to feel as if
my whole body is filled
with the radiant light of healthy vitality;
on every level of my being
there is perfect balance and integrity;
and my capacity for love, wisdom,
right actions and healing
is growing every day.

Thanks be to God.

‡

A Prayer Of Relaxation

~

First, before I enter the sacred space,
I know my heart and mind are open.

Then, and only then, I am ready to go within.

I find myself inside, surrendering all to the Divine.

And now
with the reverence due to their sacred essence
I read the words of this prayer, feeling their truth
resonating deeply
in the core of my being
and a spring of joy pours from my heart
that it is so.

In giving myself to this prayer,
my heart is alive with a profound and passionate longing
for that which through this prayer I create:

A Prayer Of Relaxation

I relax everything now
in mind and body
open, in the flowing
present to Now
with the One
receiving and giving
the aliveness of Love

I have always been
and am now
loved, whole,
loving and creating

With heart open
and mind open
I welcome this truth
I celebrate this truth
I embody and resonate this truth

So be it
Thank you, thank you
From my heart and soul
Thank you
Great Spirit
Creator of all Creation.

‡

A Prayer Of Living Faith

~

In my whole being:
effortless peace,
love and harmony
now and always

In my whole being:
living faith in the supreme power of love
now and always

In my whole being:
clear direct communication with God
and my spirit guides and guardian angels,
now and always

All this now and always,
inherently, constantly,
consciously and unconsciously.

I am embodied consciousness
And I am the nowhere point of consciousness

In the space-time dream
And out.

‡

In Praise Of The Silent Sound:
Prayer Of The Holy Wow

~

[Note: this prayer to be read silently, not spoken aloud.]

Within the Now
Within the now
This Now
This now
The holy Wow
The miraculous eternity of being

Within the Now
Within this miracle
This now
The now of only now
The holy Wow
AUM
The holy Wow
AUM

Within the Now
Here are the myriad finite things
This now
And the infinite
The holy Wow
AUM
Everything and no thing

Within the Now
All time and no time
This now
Creator, creation and creature
Are One
The holy Wow
AUM.

‡

This Is Enough

~

I notice, I feel, what is ready to be let go and,
with a blessing, I let it go.

There is newness here,
I notice, I feel and welcome it.

There is goodness here,
I notice, I feel and welcome it.

There is love here,
I notice, I feel and welcome it.

This is enough,
I feel gratitude for this.

‡

I Feel This And I Know It

~

I feel this and I know it
This body is supple, strong and miraculous, constantly
healing, cleansing and renewing itself,

I feel this and I know it
This mind has clarity and focus, and is miraculous,
constantly expanding its capabilities and power,

I feel this and I know it
This heart is alive with light and warmth, it is miraculous,
constantly deepening its roots
in the One True Source of Love,

I feel this and I know it
I am this soul, free, ecstatic and all-embracing, one with the
God of Love and All Creation,

I feel this and I know it.

‡

(To exist is to be now.)

~

I pray for,
in other words my heart is flaming
with a profound and passionate longing for,
and through this prayer I create, ...

A paradigm-shift
a beautiful complete simple miraculous evolutionary
quantum-leap of all human consciousness
into ever deepening, living and growing,
Peace, Love and Harmony
with God, Creation, Nature and Each Other, Now.

(To exist is to be now.)

‡

The Practice Of Love

~

Practising to do without thinking
Practising not thinking
Loving this practice
Loving this life.

‡

Interbeing Invocation

~

All In One, In All, In One,
One In All, In One, In All,
All In One ......

Help me to clear my body
So that it may resonate in harmony
With the energy of
Your Unlimited Power

Help me to clear my mind
So that it may resonate in harmony
With the energy of
Your Transcending Wisdom, All-Seeing, All-Knowing

Help me to clear my heart
So that it may resonate in harmony
With the energy of
Your Eternal Love, Divine Love, Pure Love,
All-Embracing Love

Help me to clear my soul
So that it may resonate in harmony
With the energy of
The One In All, All In One, In All, In One

* * * *

My body is clear
And it is
Resonating in harmony
With the energy of
Your Unlimited Power

My mind is clear
And it is
Resonating in harmony
With the energy of
Your Transcending Wisdom, All-Seeing, All-Knowing

My heart is clear
And it is
Resonating in harmony
With the energy of
Your Eternal Love, Divine Love, Pure Love,
All-Embracing Love

My soul is clear
And it is
Resonating in harmony
With the energy of
The All in Onc, One in All,
In One, In All

* * * *

My body is clear
My mind is clear
My heart is clear
My soul is clear

And my Whole Being is
Resonating in harmony
With the energy of
Power, Wisdom, Love, Truth,
The All in One, One in All,
In One, In All,
All In One ......

‡

Everything I Know

~

All, all, all.
My mother and father,
My brothers and sisters,
All my ancestors,
All the born and unborn,
My very life and being,
Which although I call it mine,
Really there is nothing to own
And no one to own it!

All, all, all,
Everything and nothing,
Everything I know,
Everything I don't know,
Everything I am,
Every thing here,
Everything I'm feeling,
Every thing now,
Every thought,
Every action,
Every place,
Every empty space,

All, all, all is infused with,
Is within and inseparable from:
All-Knowing, All-Seeing,
Supreme Intelligence,
Divine Love,

Divine Mother and Father,
Divine One,
The Living Creator,
The Eternal Now,
The un-nameable Tao;

Beyond all innocence
And all wisdom,
Beyond all dualities,
All simplicities and complexities,
Beyond the understanding of the thinking mind:
In every cell in every body,
There lives, and always has lived,
A most profound knowing,
A most profound truth:
All in One, One in All.
All in One, One in All.
All in One, One in All.

I Am This Truth.
May I feel this truth in my heart,
May I live this truth in my life.
I Am This Truth.

‡

Wadiz was the caterpillar, Sounds-of-Wings now is the butterfly.

THE KEY

Song lyrics

Look Again And See

~

Are you searching for the key?
No need to search any more
Look again, look and see
There is no lock on this door

Are you waiting to be invited?
No need to wait any more
Look again, look and see
This is an always open door

Are you wondering, 'Is this my rightful place?'
No need to wonder any more
Look again, look and see
Really, there is no door

Who knows your purpose here?
You can be sure
When you look, you will see
You are already in the Garden

This is your home
The flowers are in their finest
The trees are trembling with excitement
The birds are singing in celebration
You are most welcome here

Come now into the presence
Of the King and Queen.

All We Can Say

~

This human life is like a bridge
A place where earth and sky can meet
And here is time and timelessness
Come together, how can this be?

I do my best but I confess
To understand is beyond me
So let the mind be calm and rest
This life is more, much more than words

For these divisions and separations
Are just a play, the mind's illusions
In real life, I'm not a bridge
There is no earth, there is no sky

All we can say is All is One
And One is All, and All is One
And yet of all, there is none
And here there is no-one.

§

The Garden Of The Heart

~

God gives you every day
This miracle of life
But it's not really yours
Unless you know yourself
Yourself as God

Devoted students of Nature
Are learning to stop making noise
They turn the sound of their lives
Into thanks and praise
For this home of the heart

We all live in the Garden
The Garden of the Heart
Devoted students
Learning listening
To be in harmony

Sing with all your body
Sing with all your heart
When you know this Love
Giving thanks and praise
Happens spontaneously

Dance with all your body
Dance with all your heart
When you know this Love
Giving thanks and praise
Happens spontaneously.

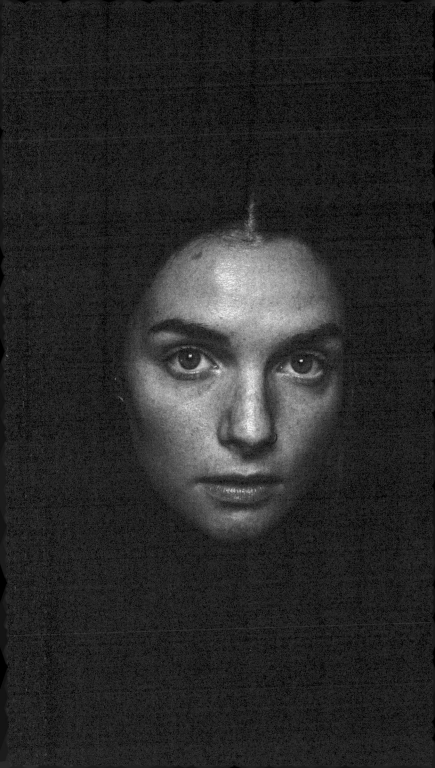

You Make Your Life

~

Here is my true home
The Garden of Love
It's what I carry
Deep in my heart
Give to the garden
Where love is growing
O my heart open
Open, open!

I am a gardener
I work uprooting
The weeds of doubt
And fearfulness
Singing is giving
Giving is healing
Give to the garden
Garden of Love

Delight in beauty
For this is serving
The sacred union
Of Heaven and Earth
Tending the green shoots
Harvesting ripe fruits
The happiness
Of living love

You are the sunlight
You are the moonlight
Fresh air and water
And fertile earth
In these life-giving
Elemental wonders
You make your life
You make your life.

§

Weary Traveler

~

Weary traveler
Welcome
Come in
Let me wash your feet

Draw near
To the fire in your heart
Let the karma burn
Be revealed to yourself

A wave of love
A beam of light
A flowing of now
A song of life

This knowing of feeling
This feeling of knowing
This knowing of not knowing
Aum.

§

Of Woman

~

Of woman I am born
Of woman I am born
From this love I have my life
With this body I live
With this body I live

Brother and sister mine
Brother and sister mine
From this Love we have our life
On the Green and Blue
On the Green and Blue

Hail and praise to the Moon
Hail and praise to the Moon
Around the Earth you have your life
Around the Earth you live
Around the Earth you live

Hail and praise to the Blue
Hail and praise to the Green
Around the Sun you have your life
Around the Sun you live
Around the Sun you live

Hail and praise to the Sun
Hail and praise to the Sun
There in Space you have your life
There in Space you live
There in Space you live

Hail and praise to Space
Hail and praise to Space
Twin to Time you have your life
Twin to Time you live
Twin to Time you live

Hail and praise to the One
Hail and praise to the One
All in One you have your life
One in All you live
One in All you live

Hail and praises sing
Hail and praises sing
From One Love I have Myself
As one love i live
As one love i live.

§

Beauty

~

Beauty is in the way you look
And in the way you are seen
Resonance there is
Between the way you look
And the way you are seen

Beauty is in the way you love
And in the way you are loved
Resonance there is
Between the way you love
And the way you are loved

Beauty is in how you forgive
And in the way you receive
Resonance there is
Between how you forgive
And the way you receive

Beauty is in how you are now
And in how you are always
Resonance there is
Between how you are now
And how you are always.

§

Surrender My Heart

~

Surrender my heart
And clear the pathways
Open the gates
Welcome to here

The love of God
In all creation

In my mother, in my father,
In the baby and in me.

§

Yes There Is No Path

~

Yes I am clearing my way
Yes I am on my path
Yes there are no obstructions
Yes there is no path
Yes there is no path

Yes there are no obstructions
Yes there is no path
Yes I am clearing my way
Yes I am on my path
Yes I am on my path.

§

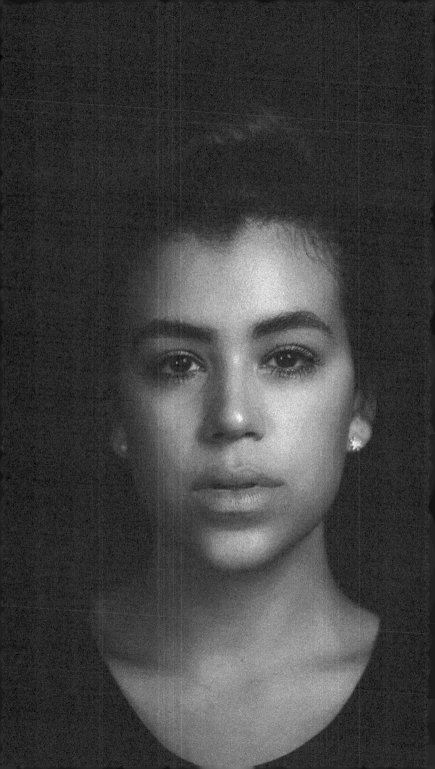

The Flower of Love

~

I love to sing with you
I love to dance with you
I love to be with you
I love you

Here I remember
The meaning of a prayer
Is brought into being
Through my heart

The energy of love is
Here and now alive
I bring my aliveness
To bring this prayer to life

Taking courage
To feel the truth of
The unifying power
Of an open heart

Being on the inside of
This coming together
Living connections
Deepening

With Trust in my Creator
The One in All
The God of Love
And all Creation

I am here and you are there
Apparent separation
But what are we
In reality?

We are nothing other than
Petals of the Living One
Ever-blossoming
Flower of Love.

§

Attune Your Receptivity

~

Now is the time
Give your chattering mind
A much needed rest
It's been doing too much

Turn your mind to peace
Just what it needs
Make a good start
Feel trust in your heart

There is more to life
More to life than words
Fine tune into
Your heart guiding you

Attune to the subtle vibrations
Feel what's alive
There is a lot going on
Attend to your intention

Captain of your ship
Keep to the present and the real
God made these for you
Show your gratitude

Feel what's alive
In the physical
And the emotional
And the astral

Attune your receptivity
Don't know anything
Attune your receptivity
Don't know anything

Attune your receptivity
Feeling what's alive
Attune your receptivity
Feeling what's alive.

§

Unmoor Your Boat

~

Unmoor, unmoor your boat
Ah yes, the sailing boat
Untie, be taken

Untie, untie be taken
In Nature's embrace
Of joy, of life

She gives, she gives
She gives birth
And loves you forever

Bearer, bearer
Birther, birther
Mother, of all

Dearest, dearest Mother
Beautiful beyond compare
Powerful beyond,
Beyond measure

I worship and honour You
My life is really yours
We dance and sing
For joy,
For life, for love.

§

Keep It Simple

~

I was sick then I was well
Now I am as I am
Everything a gift from God
So I keep it very simple

We are here as finite beings
Dancing with infinity
Every day your first and last
Keep Heart and Mind in unity

Awe and wonder everywhere
The Heart was made for loving
Smiling might be seen
Or tears falling

One task: to make my way
Being true in gratitude
For all that was, is now, shall be
As I look so I can see

Divine Love is here in us
In this healing
Just as we are now
Just as it is

So I keep it very simple,
I trust the Maker of this life
All my faith is in Love
I keep my flame of faith alight.

§

This Is It

~

This is it
It is changing
This is it
It is unchanging

It is All in One
OM, OM, OM

This is it
It is non-existent
This is it
It is Three and Four in One

It is All in One
OM, OM, OM

We come from love
Live with love
Return to love
I am in love

We are All in One
OM, OM, OM

We come from One
Live with All
Return to One
I am in All

We are All in One
OM, OM, OM

§

Love Is The Answer

~

Light and reflections
All colours and vibrations
Sounds in waves
Gaia dances

Om Om

Her beauty unbounded
Unlimited, ineffable
Great Spirit is Unchanging

Clear direct communion
Through my heart with my spirit guides
Living faith in the supreme
Power of love

Love is the answer
What is your question?
Love is the answer.

§

In Love With Life

~

Let the body release
Let the mind be open
Let the heart be open

Feel in love
Feel in love
Feel in love with life
Just as, just as
Just as it is

Body releasing
Mind opening
Heart opening

Growing love
Growing peace
Growing happiness
Just like
Just like
Just like this.

§

With This Sacred Breath

~

With this sacred breath I pray
With this prayer I free my heart
O my Mother, O my Father
Thank you for your gift of life

From the trees I learn to stand
From the leaves I learn to fall
How I love this living beauty
Awe and wonder everywhere

Power animals and plants
In truth and wisdom you abide
From the deep of the wild
Growing strength and light inside

In communion with my guardians
Now I breathe and now I see
My soul lives in blissful union
One eternal harmony.

§

Here Are The Stars

~

Here are the stars and the sun
And the planets and the moon
And the Earth
Here is the soul and the heart
And the body and the mind
In the Now

Let there be light, let there be
Love and truth, let there be
Peace on Earth
Let there be peace in my mind
Let there be love and joy
In my life

I feel the power of the truth
And the beauty and the love
Of my Creator
I am alive here and now
Singing praises, giving thanks
To my Creator.

§

Photo Credits

3	Houcine Ncib
7	Banjo Emerson Mathew
13	Zulmaury Saavedra
19	Caique Silva
25	Ethan Haddox
31	Jabari Timothy
37	Fethi Bouhaouchine
45	Alexander Krivitskiy
59	Brad Lloyd
71	Abdullah Ali
87	Cristian Newman
91	Dibakar Roy
97	Mahdi Asadi
107	Johan M Zacharia
111	Quinten de Graaf
115	Lalithmalhaar Gudi
121	João Paulo de Souza
127	Lilawa Studio
137	Dana Katharina
143	Carl Nenzén Lovén

All photos public domain via Unsplash

Epilogue - The Secret Knowledge

~

As has been written,
as has been foretold,
the signs are clear,
it is now the time.

The secret knowledge,
closely guarded,
and passed only to chosen ones
from generation to generation
across thousands of years,
that I reveal to you now,
is that there is no secret knowledge.

Know that peace,
liberty and love
are your birthright;
claim what is yours,
for one and all.

§

ESOTERIC

The Six Sacred Threads In
The Helix Of Our Humanity

~

Breathe and relax
Feel trust and love,
Forgiveness and compassion

Om Mani Padme Hum
Om Mani Padme Hum
Om Mani Padme Hum
Om Mani Padme Hum

Ask in love and receive in love
Work, rest and play
Dance, sing and pray

Om Mani Padme Hum
Om Mani Padme Hum
Om Mani Padme Hum
Om Mani Padme Hum.

§

Lightning Source UK Ltd.
Milton Keynes UK
UKHW021834071021
391827UK00006B/63

9 781526 209009